BREAD

FOR HUNGRY CHRISTIANS

Frank Hamrick & Jerry Dean

PositiveAction
BIBLE CURRICULUM

BREAD: FOR HUNGRY CHRISTIANS
written by Frank Hamrick and Jerry Dean

Copyright 1977, 2009, 2013 by Positive Action for Christ, Inc.,
P.O. Box 700, 502 W. Pippen St., Whitakers, NC 27891.

Third Edition 2013
Second Printing 2017

Printed in the United States of America

ISBN: 978-1-59557-173-1

Edited by C.J. Harris
Designed by Shannon Brown

Published by

TABLE OF CONTENTS

And Jesus said unto them, I am the bread of life: he that cometh to Me shall never hunger; and he that believeth on Me shall never thirst.

John 6:35

Bread is a nearly universal staple. From the dawn of time, almost every human civilization has depended on bread as an efficient, reliable way to sustain life in communities big or small.

It's significant that Jesus Christ presented Himself as bread that came down from heaven (John 6:51). As the children of Israel hungered in the wilderness and found manna sent from the Father, so also is a person's soul satisfied by Jesus Christ, the true and living Bread. The world searches for that which can bring peace and contentment, and still there is restlessness within. They seek and find not. They thirst and find no refreshment for their parched, dry souls. Only Christ Jesus, the Bread of Life, can quench the thirst and fill the heart of an unregenerate person. Only He can fill the void caused by sin.

This booklet is a study of our Savior. It is written for those who are hungry for the things of God. In Matthew 5 we read that blessed are those who hunger and thirst after righteousness, because they will be filled. As you read and study the life of Christ, it is our desire that you will see Him in a new light and that He will become dearer and more precious to you. Christ has done more than our mortal minds can ever comprehend, yet the Word provides us with a beautiful picture of His life, death, and present work. To the Christian, He truly is Bread, the daily sustenance.

Before you begin your study, however, why not pause and ask God to give you a fresh look at His Son and His finished work. Ask Him to thrill your heart anew with the wonderful salvation and joyous, abundant life He has provided in Himself. May God bless you as you study His infallible Word.

1

CHRIST:
HIS PRE-EXISTENCE

In this chapter we will study the preincarnate Christ.

> *What does preincarnate mean?*

The word *preincarnate* is really two words put together. *Pre* means before. *Incarnate* means in the flesh. Thus, the preincarnation of Christ speaks of the time before Christ came in the flesh to Earth.

> *Since Christ is called the Son of God,*
> *wasn't He created by God?*

Let's see what the Bible says about Christ's pre-existence—that is, before He came to Earth.

CREATOR AND SUSTAINER

- We have already studied this verse in the *Meat* booklet, but look again at Genesis 1:26. Does God refer to Himself in the singular, or in the plural? _____ What do you think that means? _____ _____ _____

We have seen in our study of the Trinity and the Holy Spirit that God's Spirit aided in creation.

> *But that doesn't mean Christ helped, as well.*

- Turn to John 1:1–2. Who is the Word mentioned in these verses? See also verse 14. _____

- Now look at verse 3. What did He do? _____ _____

- Turn to Hebrews 1:2. According to this verse, by whom did God create the world?_____

- Now read Colossians 1:15–17. What does this passage state about Christ?_____ _____ _____

- Notice especially verse 17. What two things are said about Christ?

  1. _____

     _____

  2. _____

     _____

- All things are held together, or consist, by Christ. What does this fact teach us about Him? _____

  _____

  _____

Christ is the Creator and Sustainer of the universe.

> *But couldn't Christ have been created before
> the world was created?*

FROM EVERLASTING TO EVERLASTING

- Turn to John 1:1–2. In your own words, what do these verses plainly state about Christ? _____

  _____

  _____

- Now look at Micah 5:2. Though Christ was born in Bethlehem, did He begin there? _____

- How long has He existed? _____

  _____

- See also John 17:5. How does Christ ask God to glorify Him? _____

  _____

  _____

Jesus also claimed His own pre-existence.

- Look at Exodus 3:14. God is giving Moses instructions so that he will be accepted by the Israelites as their leader. Who did God tell Moses to say sent him? _____

The Hebrew word for "I am" is a name for God that was so revered and holy that the Jews would not even speak it!

- Now look at John 8:58. What did Jesus say here?

  _____

- What did He mean by that? _____

  _____

  _____

  _____

- In verses 58–59, how did the people respond when Jesus equated Himself with God?_____

  _____

- Turn to Revelation 1:8. What did Christ say regarding Himself in this verse? _____

  _____

  _____

  _____

The Scriptures plainly teach that Jesus Christ, the Son of God, has existed with and in the Father in eternity past and in the present, and He will continue to do so in the future. He is equal with God in every respect. He merely lowered Himself, taking the form of a human being so that you and I might be redeemed. What a great God and Savior we have!

Complete This Section Without Looking Back at the Lesson

1. Define preincarnation. _____

   _____

   _____

2. What does John 1:1–3 teach concerning Christ?

   _____

   _____

   _____

3. What two things does Colossians 1:17 teach us about Christ? _____

_____

_____

_____

4. According to John 17:5, what did Christ share with the Father in eternity past? _____

_____

5. What did Jesus mean when He said, "I am"?

_____

_____

_____

_____

Verses to Memorize

- Colossians 1:16–17
- John 8:58

2
CHRIST:
HIS VIRGIN BIRTH

What is the virgin birth?

When we say that Christ was born of a virgin, we mean that He was born of a woman, but He had no human father.

Does the Bible really teach the virgin birth?

First, let's look at prophetic Scripture.

DOOM PRONOUNCED ON MANKIND

Turn to Genesis 3:14–15. Here we read the very first prophecy in the Bible.

- To whom is the Lord God speaking? _____
- Who is the serpent? _____
- Who is the woman in verse 15? _____
- What would be the attitude of the devil and the woman toward each other from this point on? _____
  _____

- But notice the latter part of verse 15. The verse says that there will not only be conflict between the serpent and the woman but also between whom? _____
  _____

- Who do you think is the woman's offspring, or seed, mentioned in verse 15? _____
  _____

- So there would also be conflict between whom?
  _____

A DELIVERER PROMISED

Now notice the pronoun "her" in verse 15. This is a key word. Everywhere else in the Bible a different pronoun is used when speaking of descendants. Look up these verses: Genesis 46:6, Psalm 18:50, Isaiah 53:10.

- What pronoun is used in each verse? _____

- We can see by these verses that there was to be a future descendant of Eve who would be different from all other humans. He would be of the seed, or offspring, of woman and not of man. The rest of Genesis 3:15 tells us what this unique individual would do. First, whose head would be bruised, or crushed? _____

- Now, notice again the personal pronoun in the last phrase of verse 15. What will Satan do to the seed, or offspring, of the woman? _____

  _____

  So, we see here that the seed of the woman is a person who will bruise the head of Satan.

> *What does it mean to bruise someone's head?*

- Christ mortally bruised Satan when He died on Calvary and rose again the third day. Christ has brought victory over the devil. But the key point to keep in mind is that Christ is the seed, or offspring, of _____. This prophesies the virgin birth.

- Turn to another prophetic Scripture, Isaiah 7:14. In this passage it is plainly stated that a virgin shall conceive and bear a son. What is the child's name? _____

- Now turn to Matthew 1:23–25. Who is this prophesied virgin-born child? _____

- Notice also what Luke, a very competent physician, says in Luke 1:30–38. What does the key verse (37) say?

  _____

  _____

> *What difference does it make? Christ could be the*
> *Savior and not be virgin-born, couldn't He?*

THE BIBLE'S CREDIBILITY HINGES ON IT

- If Christ were not born of a virgin, how would that affect the reliability of the Scriptures? _____

  _____

  _____

CHRIST'S SINLESSNESS IS A FACTOR

- You may remember that we studied the doctrine of anthropology, or mankind, in the *Meat* booklet. Briefly, in your own words, what does Romans 5:12–14 mean?

  _____

  _____

  _____

- Every descendant of Adam has sinned. We've already seen that another word for descendant is what (Gen. 3:15)?

  _____

- Since Christ was not of the seed, or offspring, of Adam, does Romans 5:12 apply to Him? _____

- Why or why not?_____

  _____

  _____

  _____

  _____

> *Since Christ wasn't born of the seed of man, He didn't inherit Adam's sinful nature. Therefore, Christ is the only human ever who wasn't a sinner!*

- In your own words, what does 2 Corinthians 5:21 tell us about Christ?_____

  _____

  _____

  _____

- State what 1 Peter 3:18 means to those who are God's children. _____
_____
_____
_____

> *If Christ had been born naturally, He would have been a sinner, and He couldn't have died for anyone else's sins.*

Christ's virgin birth makes it possible for us to have a sinless, perfect Savior who could die in our place for our sins.

Complete This Section Without Looking Back at the Lesson

1. Define virgin birth. _____
_____
_____

2. What does Genesis 3:15 tell us about the relationship between the seed, or offspring, of the woman and the seed of the serpent? _____
_____
_____
_____

3. What did God mean when He said that Christ would bruise Satan's head? _____
_____
_____

4. Why is it necessary that Christ was born of a virgin?
_____
_____
_____
_____

Verses to Memorize

- Genesis 3:15
- Isaiah 7:14

3
CHRIST:
HIS PURPOSE IN COMING

There are many views of the purpose for Christ's coming and death on the cross. Let's look first at the false views of Christ's coming and death.

UNSCRIPTURAL VIEWS OF CHRIST'S COMING AND DEATH

The Accident Theory

Christ's death was an accident. He never intended to die on a cross.

First, it was prophesied that Christ would die. Look up the following Old Testament passages and match each verse with the corresponding description of Christ's death made many years before He actually came to Earth.

1. ____ Psalm 22:6	A. Despised by the people
2. ____ Psalm 22:7	B. Rejected by men
3. ____ Psalm 22:14	C. Divided garments
4. ____ Psalm 22:15	D. Laughed to scorn; mocked
5. ____ Psalm 22:16	E. Thirty pieces of silver
6. ____ Psalm 22:18	F. Wounded for our sins
7. ____ Isaiah 53:3	G. Bones out of joint
8. ____ Isaiah 53:4	H. Pierced hands and feet
9. ____ Isaiah 53:5	I. With rich in death
10. ____ Isaiah 53:7	J. Lamb led to slaughter
11. ____ Isaiah 53:9	K. Smitten, punished by God
12. ____ Zechariah 11:12	L. Tongue sticks to mouth

- What do these Scriptures prove about Christ's coming?

  _____

  _____

  _____

- Notice also that Christ talked about His coming death. Read Matthew 16:21, Mark 9:30–32, and John 10:17–18 and state in your own words what Christ said.

_____

_____

_____

- If Christ knew so much about His death and resurrection beforehand, could it have been an accident?_____

The Martyr Theory

> *Christ was killed because He was faithful to His principles and to what He considered His duty. From Him we can learn faithfulness to truth and duty. His example can teach us to repent of our sins and to reform.*

This view of Christ's death teaches that salvation comes through following the example of Christ.

- Look up the following verses and state how we are saved.

1. Ephesians 2:8a _____

    _____

2. 1 Peter 1:18–19 _____

    _____

3. John 1:12 _____

    _____

- In the following verses we are told to follow Christ's example (1 John 2:6; 1 Pet. 2:21, 24; Matt. 11:29). To whom were these verses written? _____

- Is it possible for an unsaved person to follow Christ's perfect example? _____

- Why or why not? Give Scripture to support your answer.

_____

_____

_____

_____

- If Christ was nothing more than a martyr, then His death is no more meaningful than Stephen's—or that of any other martyr. In Acts 4:12, what does Peter say about Christ that proves Christ's death to be more than simple martyrdom? _____

The Governmental Theory

The benevolence of God requires that He make an example of suffering in Christ to show us that sin is displeasing in His sight. God's government of the world requires a display of His wrath against sin.

- It is true that God is displeased with the sin of mankind. But what kind of person did God choose to show His displeasure against sin? See 2 Corinthians 5:21 and 1 Peter 3:18.

If God wanted only to show His displeasure for the sins of the human race, why would He choose His divine, innocent Son, not a guilty human?

The Love of God Theory

Christ died just to show people how much God loved them. From then on they would know how God felt toward them. He died to communicate humanity's real worth to God.

It's true that God demonstrated His love by sending Christ to die (Rom. 5:8; John 3:16), but people did not need such a sacrifice to know that God loved them. They should have known this before Christ came. Psalm 103 is just one of many songs of praise to God for His love, and it was written long before the time of Christ.

- Look again at 2 Corinthians 5:21. Why does this verse say Christ was made sin for us'? _____
_____
_____

- What reason does 1 Peter 3:18 give for Christ's death?

  _____

  _____

  _____

Christ's death reveals God's love, but God's love is not the reason for Christ's death.

BIBLICAL REASONS FOR CHRIST'S COMING AND DEATH

Now let's see the biblical reasons for Christ's coming.

He Came to Fulfill the Promises of God

- After each reference, list the prophecy that Christ fulfilled.

  1. Genesis 3:15

     _____

  2. Isaiah 7:14

     _____

  3. Micah 5:2

     _____

  4. Isaiah 9:6

     _____

  5. Zechariah 11:13–14

     _____

  6. Isaiah 53:12

     _____

He Came to Reveal the Father

- State in your own words what John 1:18 and 14:9 mean.

  _____

  _____

  _____

He Came to Become a Faithful High Priest

Christ came in the flesh so that He could understand our condition, situation, and temptations—and so be qualified as a faithful High Priest.

- Read Hebrews 5:1–2 and write in your own words how and why the Old Testament high priests were chosen.

  - _____
    _____
    _____

- As you understand it, what does Hebrews 2:17–18 mean?
  _____
  _____

- And what does Hebrews 4:15–16 mean? _____
  _____
  _____
  _____

He Came to Put Away Sin

- Read Hebrews 9:26. What does the end of the verse say that Christ did? _____
  _____
  _____

- Turn to 1 John 3:5. What does this verse mean?
  _____
  _____
  _____

- What does Mark 10:45 say was Christ's purpose in coming to Earth? _____
  _____
  _____

He Came to Destroy the Works of the Devil

- Read 1 John 3:8b and state why the Son of God was manifested. _____
  _____
  _____

- What does Hebrews 2:14–15 mean? _____
  _____
  _____
  _____

He Came to Give Us an Example of a Holy Life

- Though Christ did not state explicitly that He came to give us an example, that purpose is strongly implied in the Scriptures. What do the following verses instruct us to do?

  - 1 John 2:6 _____
    _____

  - 1 Peter 2:21 _____
    _____

He Came to Prepare for the Second Coming

The sacrifice of Christ saves us now from the power, penalty, and guilt of sin. Yet you and I are still forced to exist in this sinful world, with all of its temptations and evil. Christ's salvation assures us that He will one day return and rapture the redeemed unto Himself, freeing us finally from the very presence of sin.

- How does Paul describe his earthly condition and heavenly hope in Romans 8:22–23? _____
  _____
  _____
  _____
  _____

1. List the four false views of Christ's coming and death, and then refute each with Scripture.

    - _____
      _____
      _____

    - _____
      _____
      _____
      _____

    - _____
      _____
      _____

    - _____
      _____
      _____

2. List the seven reasons Christ came to Earth to die, and then give Scripture to prove your answer.

    - _____
      _____
      _____

    - _____
      _____
      _____

    - _____
      _____
      _____

    - _____
      _____
      _____

- _____
  _____
- _____
  _____
  _____
- _____
  _____
  _____

Verses to Memorize

- Hebrews 4:15
- 2 Corinthians 5:21

4

CHRIST:
HIS CHARACTER

> *What kind of person was Christ?*
> *What made Him so different from other people?*

The Bible is quite clear as to Christ's character—the kind of person He really was in everyday life. Let's look at the character of the Savior.

CHRIST WAS HOLY

- He was called holy. Look up the following verses and write beside each the biblical title given to Christ.

    1. Mark 1:24 _____

    2. Luke 1:35 _____

    3. Luke 2:23 _____

    4. Acts 2:27 _____

    5. Acts 3:14 _____

    6. Acts 4.27 _____

    7. Acts 4:30 _____

> *What does the word holy mean anyway?*

- In your own words, write a definition of the word *holy*.

    _____

    _____

    _____

- Find a dictionary. How does it define *holy*?

    _____

    _____

    _____

In reference to Christ, the word *holy* means perfect, sinless, without fault. He had a holy nature. Look at John 14:30 and answer the following questions.

- Who is speaking? _____
- Who is the prince and ruler of this world? _____
- In your own words, what does the last phrase mean?

  _____

  _____

  _____

- The last phrase actually means that Satan had absolutely no power over any phase of Christ's nature and life. We have already seen how the devil can control other people, but to Christ he can do nothing. What phrase in Hebrews 4:15 further proves Christ's holy nature?

  _____

He was holy in conduct. Hebrews 7:26 states that Christ was separate, or set apart, from sinners.

- What does this mean? _____

  _____

  _____

Christ never followed the ways of mankind. He never sinned. He always did those things that pleased His Father.

- Read John 8:29b. What does the verse mean?

  _____

  _____

CHRIST HAD GENUINE LOVE

- Look up the following passages, and write down who Christ loved and how that love was revealed.

  1. John 15:13; Romans 5:8 _____

     _____

     _____

  2. Ephesians 5:2, 25 _____

     _____

     _____

3. John 15:9 _____

_____

4. Luke 23:32–36; Matthew 5:43–48 _____

_____

_____

CHRIST WAS HUMBLE

- Look up the verses below, and state in your own words how Christ humbled Himself.

    1. Philippians 2:5–8 _____

    _____

    _____

    2. 2 Corinthians 8:9 _____

    _____

    3. Luke 2:7 _____

    _____

    4. Luke 9:58 _____

    _____

    5. Matthew 20:28 _____

    _____

    6. John 13:14 _____

    _____

HE HAD A MEANINGFUL, CONSISTENT PRAYER LIFE

- When did Christ pray?

    1. Luke 6:12 _____

    2. Mark 1:35 _____

    3. Matthew 26:38–46_____

    4. John 6:15–16 _____

If Christ, the holy Son of God, needed to pray so much, what about us?

HE WORKED STEADILY AT WHAT GOD HAD FOR HIM TO DO

- State in your own words what Christ meant in John 9:4.

  _____

  _____

  _____

- When did Christ's day begin (Mark 1:35; John 8:2)?

  _____

- When did it end (Matt. 8:16; John 3:2)? _____

  _____

- When Christ was doing God's work, what things did He sometimes neglect or disregard?

  1. John 4:31–34 _____

  2. Mark 6:31–34 _____

  3. Luke 23:40–43 _____

> *What difference does it make?*
> *I can't be like Christ—He was God!*

- Read 1 Peter 2:21 and 1 John 2:6. What are we instructed to do? _____

- In Galatians 4:19, what was Paul's desire for the Christians of Galatia? _____

  _____

- What do you think he meant? _____

  _____

> *But how can I be like Christ?*

In John 15, Christ presents Himself as the true vine and Christians as the branches. We must remember that only Christ, our Life, can give us the power and strength to follow His steps. We must abide, or remain, in Him. Each day, we must focus our minds and thoughts on Him. As we seek Him, God provides the guidance and strength to overcome our sinful flesh and follow Him.

- Read Galatians 5:22–23. As we yield to the Holy Spirit, what characteristics of Christ will be produced in our lives?

  _____

  _____

  _____

Have you surrendered your life to the Lord today? Are you as close to the Lord as you once were? Why not kneel, right now, and confess your sins to the Lord, yielding your body anew to His control.

Complete This Section Without Looking Back at the Lesson

1. What are the five elements of Christ's character that you studied in this chapter?

   - _____

   - _____

   - _____

   - _____

   - _____

2. What does the word *holy* mean? _____

   _____

   _____

3. In what ways was Christ holy? _____

   _____

   _____

4. What verse proves that Christ demonstrated His love for sinners by dying for them? _____

5. Where do we get the strength to live a life of Christlikeness? _____

   _____

Verses to Memorize

- 1 Peter 2:21
- John 15:4

5

CHRIST:
HIS SINLESS LIFE

> *Yes, the Bible calls Christ holy, but that doesn't really mean He was sinless. Why is it so important that Christ didn't sin?*

- We have studied the deity of Christ in the *Meat* booklet, and in the *Bread* booklet we have studied Christ's character, virgin birth, and purpose for coming to Earth. State in your own words the answer to the following question: "Why must Christ be sinless?" Use Scripture to support your answer. _____

  _____

  _____

  _____

  _____

MORE THAN HOLY

- The Bible says that Christ was more than just holy. Look up the following verses and list the word or words that reveal Christ's character.

  1. Isaiah 53:9 _____
  2. Isaiah 53:11 _____
  3. Zechariah 9:9 _____
  4. Matthew 27:3–4 _____
  5. John 5:30 _____
  6. John 7:18 _____
  7. John 8:46 _____
  8. Acts 22:14 _____
  9. 2 Corinthians 5:21_____
  10. Hebrews 1:9 _____
  11. Hebrews 7:26 _____
  12. James 1:13–14 _____
  13. 1 Peter 1:19 _____
  14. 1 Peter 2:22 _____
  15. 1 John 5:20 _____

> *Yes, but Christ is God. Sin and temptations didn't affect Him like they do me.*

- Turn to Hebrews 4:15. Who is the High Priest?

  _____

- In your own words, what does the latter part of the verse mean? _____

  _____

  _____

  _____

> *But why did Christ allow Himself to be tested and tempted so greatly?*

- Look at Hebrews 2:16–18. According to verse 16a, in what form could Christ have come to Earth?

  _____

- What form did Christ choose to take when He came to Earth? _____

  _____

- According to verse 17, why was it important for Christ to be made like other people? _____

  _____

  _____

  _____

Look closely at verse 18. Here it says Christ was tempted so He could be a help to those who are tempted.

- Now explain verses 16–18 in your own words.

  _____

  _____

  _____

  _____

  _____

  _____

> *So Christ came and lived in the flesh, suffering the same temptations I do, so He would better understand my problems? It's hard to believe He'd do that for me.*

Christ lived in this sin-cursed world, tempted on every hand so He would understand our feelings and be a faithful High Priest.

Have you thanked God recently for His faithful Son, who not only died, but lived on Earth for you—without succumbing to sin? Why not stop a moment and thank Him?

Complete This Section Without Looking Back at the Lesson

1. Why is it necessary to our faith that Christ be sinless?
   _____
   _____
   _____

2. List six references that show Christ's sinlessness.

   • _____
   • _____
   • _____
   • _____
   • _____
   • _____

3. Why did Christ allow Himself to be tempted and tested by sin? _____
   _____
   _____

4. What verse states Christ was tempted in all the ways we are?
   _____

5. What does it mean that Christ is able to help those who are tempted? _____
   _____

Verse to Memorize

- Hebrews 2:18

6

CHRIST:
HIS DEATH

- Let's go back to Genesis 2:17. What was God's command?

  _____

  _____

  _____

- What was the penalty for disobedience?_____

- In the *Meat* booklet, we learned that every person has followed Adam's rebellious example. What verses state that every person is a sinner by nature?

  _____

- Since Eden, what has God demanded as a payment for sin? _____

- Could God justly forgive any sin without requiring the death of the sinner?_____

So again we see the terrible plight of sinful humanity—lost and condemned to die, with no hope of escape.

But there is hope—in Christ!

THE VICARIOUS ATONEMENT

Now we can begin to see the importance of Christ's death. As guilty sinners, we needed a righteous substitute to take our place. In Christ we have that vicarious atonement.

Vicarious atonement—what does that mean?

- Look up the word *vicar* in the dictionary and give a one-word definition. _____

Thus we have a substitute atonement in Jesus Christ.

But what does atonement mean?

- Turn to Romans 5 and read verses 8–11. When did God demonstrate, or show, His love toward us?

  _____

- Look closely at verses 9 and 10. How does verse 9 say that sinners are justified? _____

  _____

- How does verse 10 say that God's enemies were reconciled to Himself? _____

  _____

The two words mentioned above could be defined like this:

1. Justified—made innocent of all sin
2. Reconciled—restored to favor with God

- Look at verse 11. What have we received through Christ?

  _____

- So what did Christ do to provide us with atonement and reconciliation?_____

  _____

Vicarious atonement is the act whereby Christ substituted for the sinner, paying the price for that sinner, bringing forgiveness from a holy God, and making peace with Him. No one and nothing else could have accomplished this. God's justice demanded death, and Christ satisfied that demand.

CHRIST'S DEATH IS THE BASIS OF THE GOSPEL

- Read 1 Corinthians 15:1–3, noting especially verse 1a. What is Paul telling the Corinthians about?

  _____

- Since Paul is sharing the gospel—the good news of salvation—what is the very first thing he mentions in verse 3?

  _____

Paul realized that Christ's death for sinners was the basis of the gospel message.

- Turn to Revelation 5:8–10. Who is the Lamb? _____
- What is the new song that the saved will sing throughout eternity, according to verses 9 and 10? _____

  _____

  _____

  _____

  _____

  _____

  _____

What a picture this is! We will sing forever that Christ, the Lamb who was slain, is worthy. The death of Christ is of utmost importance on Earth and in heaven.

> *But was the way He died so important?*

- Read Hebrews 9:22. What is required for the remission, or forgiveness, of sins? _____
- According to this verse, is the manner of Christ's death important?_____
- Why? _____

  _____

  _____

WHY CHRIST DIED ON A CROSS

There are two basic reasons why Christ died on a cross and not some other way.

1. Read Genesis 4:1–4. In light of Hebrews 9:22, why did God accept Abel's offering, but reject Cain's offering?

   - _____

     _____

- Read Exodus 12:1–13. What was the token that had to be on each house to avoid the death of the oldest son? _____

- Likewise, Christ had to die in a way that would shed His blood. A natural death or a death that would not shed blood could not atone for our sins. Read Romans 5:8–9. These verses tell us that Christ died for us, but what was it about His death that justifies us?

  _____

2. A second reason Christ died on the cross is that this was the method God had chosen, the one He had prophesied thousands of years before Christ was born.

   - Read Psalm 22:1–18. Next to each verse listed, record the prophecies that describe Christ's death on the cross:

     1. Verse 1 _____
        _____

     2. Verse 7 _____
        _____

     3. Verse 14 _____
        _____

     4. Verse 15 _____
        _____

     5. Verse 16 _____
        _____

     6. Verse 18 _____
        _____

This is just one of many Old Testament prophecies concerning the death of Christ. Christ had to die on the cross, not only to shed His blood, but also to fulfill the Scriptures.

- Read Mark 14:43–50. Christ stated that the soldiers had had many opportunities to capture and to kill Him, but they had not done so until now. According to this passage, what was the reason they had not captured Christ and killed Him some other way? _____

  _____

  _____

- To review, what are the two major reasons Christ died on the cross—and not some other way?

  1. _____

     _____

  2. _____

     _____

Complete This Section Without Looking Back at the Lesson

1. What is God's penalty for sin? What verses prove this fact?

   _____

   _____

2. Why did Christ have to die? _____

   _____

   _____

3. What does the word *justified* mean? _____

   _____

   _____

4. What does the word *reconciled* mean? _____

   _____

   _____

5. Define *vicarious atonement.* _____

   _____

   _____

   _____

6. What reference shows that Paul considered the death of Christ the very basis of the gospel message?

_____

7. What will be the saints' eternal song? _____

_____

8. What are the two basic reasons Christ died on a cross?

•   _____

_____

•   _____

_____

Verses to Memorize

• Romans 5:8–10

7

CHRIST:
HIS RESURRECTION

THE IMPORTANCE OF THE RESURRECTION

Many people overlook the importance of the resurrection of Christ to the Christian faith.

- Turn to 1 Corinthians 15. Notice verses 14, 17, and 18. What three things are true if Christ did not rise from the dead?

  1. _____

     _____

  2. _____

     _____

  3. _____

     _____

Some say Christ never really died, but was drugged to appear dead.

CHRIST ACTUALLY DIED

- Look up the following verses, and record the evidence showing that Christ was dead.

  1. Matthew 27:57–60 _____

     _____

     _____

  2. Mark 15:44–45 _____

     _____

     _____

  3. Mark 16:1 _____

     _____

     _____

4. John 19:32–34 _____

    _____

    _____

5. Revelation 1:4–7 _____

    _____

    _____

What facts show that Christ rose from the dead?

THE EMPTY TOMB

- Look up these verses and state the proofs for the bodily resurrection: Matthew 28:6; Mark 16:6; Luke 24:3, 12; John 20:1–2 _____

  _____

If Christ had not risen, the Romans would gladly have produced His body as evidence. But they could not—the tomb was empty.

But the disciples could have stolen the body of Jesus.

- Look at Matthew 27:62–66. What precautions did the Roman government take to keep the disciples from stealing Christ's body? _____

  _____

  _____

- Notice what took place after Christ's resurrection. Read Matthew 28:11–15, and state what happened in your own words. _____

  _____

  _____

If the disciples had stolen His body, they would have known they were preaching a hoax. Why then would they have suffered such awful martyrdom—including decapitation, crucifixion, stoning, beating, and boiling in oil—for something they knew was a hoax?

EYEWITNESS ACCOUNTS

- Read the verses below, and record who saw the Lord.

    1. Matthew 28:1–10 _____

    2. Matthew 28:16–20 _____

    3. Mark 16:9–11 _____

    4. Luke 24:34 _____

    5. Luke 24:36–43 _____

    6. John 20:26–31 _____

    7. John 21:1–6, 14 _____

    8. 1 Corinthians 15:6 _____

    9. 1 Corinthians 15:7 _____

> *Perhaps they only saw a ghost.*

- Using the following verses, describe the body of Jesus as seen by the witnesses.

    1. Luke 24:36–43 _____
    _____

    2. John 20:14 _____
    _____

    3. John 20:19 _____
    _____

    4. John 20:20 _____
    _____

    5. John 20:24–29 _____
    _____

> *What are the results of Christ's resurrection?*

- Look up the following passages, and list the results of Christ's resurrection.

  1. Acts 17:31 _____

     _____

  2. Romans 1:4 _____

     _____

  3. Romans 4:25 _____

     _____

  4. Romans 8:34 _____

     _____

  5. Ephesians 1:19–22 _____

     _____

  6. 1 Thessalonians 4:14 _____

     _____

Complete This Section Without Looking Back at the Lesson

1. What would be true if Christ did not rise from the dead?

   _____

   _____

   _____

   _____

2. What proofs can you give that Christ actually died?

   _____

   _____

   _____

   _____

   _____

3. What proves that Christ actually rose from the dead?

   _____

   _____

   _____

4. List at least five different accounts of Christ being seen alive after His resurrection, giving references for each one.

- _____
  _____

- _____
  _____

- _____
  _____

- _____
  _____

- _____
  _____

5. What proves Christ was not a ghost? _____
   _____
   _____

6. What are the six results of Christ's resurrection?

- _____
  _____

- _____
  _____

- _____
  _____

- _____
  _____

- _____
  _____

- _____
  _____

Verses to Memorize

- 1 Corinthians 15:13–14
- 1 Corinthians 15:20
- 1 Corinthians 15:55–57

8

CHRIST:
HIS ASCENSION
AND EXALTATION

The ascension was the event in which Christ departed from His disciples into heaven. The exaltation is the act whereby the risen and ascended Christ is given a place of power and honor at the Father's right hand.

CHRIST'S ASCENSION

- Look up the following passages and place them beside the correct event:

    - Mark 16:19
    - Luke 24:50–51
    - John 6:61–62
    - John 16:10
    - John 20:17
    - Acts 7:55–56
    - 1 Timothy 3:16
    - 1 Peter 3:22

  1. Christ foretells His ascension._____

     _____

  2. New Testament writers record it. _____

     _____

  3. Stephen saw the exalted Christ. _____

  4. Peter preached it._____

  5. Paul preached it. _____

- Read Acts 1:9–11. In your own words, state what happened. _____

  _____

  _____

- Read Ephesians 4:10 and Hebrews 4:14; 7:26. According to these verses, where did Christ go? _____

What is He doing now?

- Look up the following verses, and state what the ascended and exalted Christ is doing right now.

  1. John 14:2 _____

  _____

  2. Ephesians 4:10_____

  _____

  3. Hebrews 4:14–16_____

  _____

  4. Hebrews 9:24 and 1 John 2:1_____

  _____

  _____

CHRIST'S EXALTATION

What do the Scriptures say about the exaltation?

- Look up the following passages, and summarize how Christ is exalted. Some of the events below will take place in the future.

  1. 1 Corinthians 15:24–27_____

  _____

  _____

  2. Philippians 2:9–11_____

  _____

  _____

  3. Hebrews 7:24–26_____

  _____

  _____

4. Revelation 5:11–14 _____

_____

_____

• Look again at 1 Corinthians 15:24–28. According to verse 28, what will Christ do when all things are brought under His authority? _____

_____

Even in Christ's final exaltation, the glory will ultimately go to the Father. The ultimate goal of the exaltation is that God will be all in all.

> *What do Christ's ascension and*
> *exaltation mean to the Christian?*

• Look up these verses and state the results of Christ's ascension and exaltation.

1. Hebrews 4:14–16_____

_____

2. Colossians 1:18–19 _____

_____

3. Ephesians 1:20–22_____

_____

Complete This Section Without Looking Back at the Lesson

1. Define *ascension* and *exaltation*.

• Ascension _____

_____

• Exaltation _____

_____

2. List five different people who spoke of Christ's ascension and exaltation, giving a Scripture reference for each.

• _____

_____

- _____
  _____
- _____
  _____
- _____
  _____
- _____
  _____

3. Where is Christ now, and what is He doing? _____
   _____
   _____
   _____
   _____

4. What are the benefits, or results, of Christ's ascension and exaltation for the Christian?_____
   _____
   _____

Verses to Memorize

- Acts 1:10–11
- Hebrews 9:24

EXAMINATION
QUESTIONS

Answer the following questions without looking back in your book.

1. In Colossians 1:17, what does it mean that all things are held together by Christ? _____
    _____
    _____

2. Define the preincarnation of Christ._____
    _____
    _____

3. Write John 8:58 from memory. _____
    _____
    _____

4. How did Christ bruise Satan's head?_____
    _____
    _____

5. Define the virgin birth. _____
    _____
    _____

6. Why is it necessary that Christ was born of a virgin?

    •   _____
        _____
        _____

7. List seven reasons Christ came to Earth to die, giving Scripture references to prove your answers.

    •   _____
        _____
    •   _____
    •   _____
    •   _____
    •   _____
    •   _____

- _____

8. Write Isaiah 7:14 from memory. _____

_____

_____

_____

9. What verse shows that Christ demonstrated His love for sinners by dying for them? _____

10. Write Hebrews 4:15 from memory. _____

_____

_____

_____

11. What verse tells us that the seed, or offspring, of Eve will defeat Satan? _____

12. Write 2 Corinthians 5:21 from memory. _____

_____

_____

_____

13. Why is it necessary to our faith that Christ be sinless?

- _____

_____

14. What verse states that Christ was tempted in all the ways we are? _____

15. Why did Christ allow Himself to be tested and tempted by sin? _____

_____

_____

16. Define *justified*. _____

_____

_____

17. Define *reconciled*. _____

_____

_____

18. Define *vicarious atonement.* _____

_____

_____

19. List two reasons Christ died by crucifixion.

  • _____

  • _____

20. List at least five different accounts of Christ being seen alive after His resurrection, giving references for each one.

  • _____

  • _____

  • _____

  • _____

  • _____

21. What are the six results of Christ's resurrection?

  • _____

  • _____

  • _____

  • _____

  • _____

  • _____

22. Write 1 Corinthians 15:13–14 from memory._____

_____

_____

_____

23. Define *ascension* and *exaltation.* _____

_____

_____

_____

_____

24. Where is Christ now, and what is He doing? _____

_____

_____

25. Write Hebrews 9:24 from memory._____

_____

_____

_____

_____